W9-COG-437

WITHDRAWN

Just the Facts

Alternative Medicine

Claire Wallerstein

Heinemann Library
Chicago, Illinois

Customer Service 888-454-2279
Visit our website at www.heinemannlibrary.com

Designed by Jamie Asher
Originated by Ambassador Litho Ltd.
Printed and bound in China by South China Printing Company

07 06 05 04 03
10 9 8 7 6 5 4 3 2 1

Library of Congress Cataloging-in-Publication Data
Wallerstein, Claire, 1969-
  Alternative medicine / Claire Wallerstein.
      p. cm. -- (Just the facts)
Summary: Describes the increasing use of alternative medicine--including
herbal therapy, acupuncture, and meditation--as a more natural approach
than modern medicine to remedy a multitude of illnesses.
Includes bibliographical references and index.
  ISBN 1-4034-0816-5
  1. Alternative medicine--Juvenile literature. [1. Alternative
medicine.] I. Title. II. Series.
  R733 .W355 2003
  615.5--dc21

2002010935

Acknowledgments
The author and publisher are grateful to the following for permission to reproduce copyright material:
Cover photograph: meditating woman reproduced with permission of Hutchison Library; acupuncture needles with permission of Science Photo Library; homeopathic medicine with permission of MPM Images.
pp. 4–5, 7, 14 Sally and Richard Greenhill; pp. 5, 31 PA/Topham; p. 6 Maximilian Stock Ltd/Science Photo Library; p. 9 Oscar Burriel/Science Photo Library; p. 10 Dan McCoy/Rawson/Medipics; p. 11 Jean-Loup Charmet/Science Photo Library; pp. 13, 37, 41 Image Works/Topham; p. 15 Nancy Durell McKenna/Hutchison; p. 16 CC Studio/Science Photo Library; p. 17 Tom & Dee Ann McCarthy/Corbis Stockmarket; p. 18 Geoff Tomkinson/Science Photo Library; p. 19 Chapman/Topham; p. 20 Tek Image/Science Photo Library; p. 21 Andrew McClenaghan/Science Photo Library; p. 23 Tony Souter/Hutchison; p. 25 Françoise Sauze/Science Photo Library; p. 27 Elaine Thompson/Associated Press; p. 28 Bo Svane/Hodder Wayland Picture Library; p. 29 Phil Jude/Science Photo Library; p. 32 Cordelia Molloy/Science Photo Library; p. 33 Paul Biddle & Tim Malyon/Science Photo Library; p. 35 John Burbank/ Hutchison; p. 38 Hodder Wayland Picture Library; p. 43 Simon Fraser/Searle Pharmaceuticals/Science Photo Library; pp. 44, 45 Bristol Cancer Care Help Centre; p. 46 Brandenburg/FLPA; p. 47 Mark Edwards/Still Pictures; p. 49 Oxford School of Reflexology; p. 51 Josh Sher/Science Photo Library.

Every effort has been made to contact copyright holders of any material reproduced in this book. Any omissions will be rectified in subsequent printings if notice is given to the publisher.

Our special thanks to Pamela G. Richards, M.Ed., for her help in the preparation of the book.

Some words appear in bold, **like this.** You can find out what they mean by looking in the glossary.

Contents

Introduction 4
Alternative Medicine 6
History 10
Ancient Traditions 12
Who Uses What? 14
Why Is It Used? 16
Looking for Miracles 18
Types and Techniques 20
Marijuana .26
Naturopathy 28
The Role of the Media 30
Does It Work? 32
All in the Mind? 34
The Benefits 36
Curing Body and Spirit 38
The Dangers 40
Healers or Fakers? 42
The Need for Research 44
Herbs and the Environment 46
Legal Matters 48
People to Talk To 50
Information and Advice 52
More Books to Read 53
Glossary 54
Index 56

Introduction

What would you do if you had a bad headache? Maybe you would take an aspirin. Some people might prefer to use **complementary** or **alternative medicine** (CAM). They may try **acupuncture** or **hypnotherapy.** A very few might even try much stranger cures, such as sleeping on a magnetic bed or drinking a cup of their own urine.

It can be hard to put your finger on exactly what CAM is. The term lumps together hundreds of remedies, potions, treatments, and therapies. Many have little in common with each other—except that they are all different from the medical treatment usually provided by Western doctors and hospitals.

People in the United States now spend as much money on CAM as on **orthodox medicine.** In the United Kingdom, there are 50,000 CAM practitioners—twice as many as conventional doctors!

Many young people use CAM, especially those whose parents use it. The online bookstore Amazon stocks nearly 5,000 titles about alternative remedies. Many famous people swear by some form of CAM. Oscar-winning film star Halle Berry, for example, uses a lipstick containing the herb St. John's Wort to fight depression.

Popular treatments

Why is CAM so popular? One reason may be that up to 50 percent of people in rich, Western countries, such as the United States now suffer from conditions such as high blood pressure, asthma, and depression. These conditions cannot be completely cured by modern drugs. Millions of people around the world say they have gotten relief from CAM when **conventional medicine** has failed.

CAM sees illness as an imbalance in the patient's whole system. It tries to get to the underlying root cause of a health problem. The aim is to heal the person's mind, body, and spirit, rather than just his or her sore throat or stomachache.

However, if it is not used properly, CAM can sometimes do more harm than good. And with a bewildering range of pills, ointments, potions, teas, and sprays on sale, it seems harder than ever to sort the good medicine from the bad.

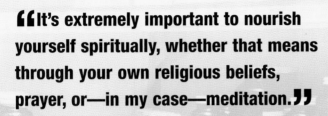

Glamorous film star Halle Berry is one of many celebrities who uses alternative therapies.

Alternative Medicine

CAM covers a wide range of healing therapies from all around the world. A few are now practiced by conventional doctors and are available in Western hospitals. However, many more remain outside the field of modern medicine and science, and have not been tested or proven in clinical trials.

Holistic treatments

Many CAM therapies are ancient, and nearly all involve a theory of **holistic treatment.** *Holistic* comes from the Greek word, "whole." It means that the whole person is being treated—his or her body, mind, and spirit. For example, a doctor may simply prescribe medicine, rest, and plenty of fluids for a person with the flu. A CAM practitioner, however, would try to deal with what caused the sickness in the first place. He or she would look at everything from the patient's diet and energy levels to any mental or emotional problems, such as stress or grief. By dealing with all of these, the aim would be to make the person stronger and more able to resist illness in the future.

Many alternative remedies are not actually what we often think of as "medicines" used to cure a disease. Many people who use them are not ill. They use CAM treatments such as vitamin supplements, **meditation,** or **yoga** as a lifestyle treatment to stay healthy over the long term. People often use several CAM therapies at the same time.

A gentler alternative?

Many of today's man-made drugs are very strong and can have negative **side effects.** CAM practitioners say their products are safer and gentler because they are natural.

However, natural does not necessarily mean safe or good. Snake venom, tobacco, arsenic, and strychnine (used in rat poison) are all natural. On the other hand, some **conventional medicines** are natural. Aspirin, for example, is derived from willow bark. Important cancer-fighting drugs come from the yew tree.

Some patients use CAM therapies as their only medical treatment. This is a real alternative to conventional medicine. More often, however, CAM is used at the same time as conventional medicine—and is **complementary.** Many people feel that neither conventional nor **alternative medicine** has all the answers, and they choose to combine the best aspects of both.

❝Alternative medicine is defined as that which cannot be tested, refuses to be tested, or consistently fails tests. If a healing technique is demonstrated to have curative properties in properly controlled trials, it ceases to be alternative. It simply becomes medicine.❞

(Biologist Richard Dawkins of Oxford University, England)

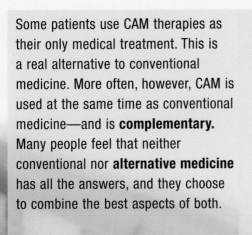

Some forms of alternative medicine may prove to cure or prevent common conditions such as the flu, which cannot be cured by conventional medicine.

7

CAM therapies

CAM therapies can be broken down into the following broad categories.

- Alternative medical systems. These include Traditional Chinese Medicine (TCM) and **Ayurveda** from India. According to these ancient systems, disease is caused by a disruption in the flow of energy around the body. They emphasize the importance of herbal remedies, diet, and the power of the body to heal itself. Although Western scientists do not believe that our bodies have any invisible energy channels, both of these medical systems have had a great deal of success. They are used by many millions of people, both in their Asian homelands and in the West.

- Mind-body systems. These include **meditation** and **hypnosis,** which send the mind into an altered state to harness its healing power. Scientists now agree that our minds have much more power over our physical health than we once thought. For example, meditation could raise the levels of important chemicals in our bodies that help to fight off infection.

- Biologically-based treatments. Many CAM products and therapies, such as **herbal medicine** and **homeopathy,** involve natural compounds believed to have medicinal properties. These range from plants and herbs such as ginseng and artichoke, to non-plant products such as royal jelly (from bees) and shark cartilage.

- Manipulative and body-based methods. Some examples are **osteopathy, chiropractic,** and **yoga.** These involve bending and moving the body either to cure an illness or injury, or to keep it strong and healthy. The body can also be used to affect the mind. For example, **massage** can be extremely helpful in calming the minds of people who feel very stressed, depressed, or nervous.

- Energy therapies. **Reiki** and faith healing, for example, claim to use the practitioner as a kind of channel to send good, healing energy into the patient. Others are said to use the energy of objects such as crystals to rebalance disrupted energy levels.

Yoga was developed thousands of years ago in India. It is used by many people to improve their general health. For example, the singer Madonna is a big fan of astanga yoga, which is very energetic and requires a lot of practice.

History

Today, doctors can carry out major life-saving operations such as heart transplants and brain surgery. It is hard to believe that medicine as we know it dates back only 100 years or so. Think of **antibiotics**—something we take for granted today. These were not produced until the mid-1900s. Until then, people often died of simple infections.

Trepanning (making a hole in the skull) was a common, but dangerous, treatment used in ancient times. It is still used today in some African countries in cases of bad headaches or mental illnesses.

Our Stone Age ancestors developed the very first medicines many thousands of years ago. Through a long process of trial and error, they learned that certain plants and substances could treat and cure some diseases. Even some animals have learned this. For example, a dog will eat grass when it has an upset stomach.

Orthodox medicine

Traditional **herbal medicine** could not cure all diseases, though. So in the Middle Ages, scientists in Europe started trying to develop new, stronger, and more effective treatments. These were often based on experiments in laboratories—the beginning of today's **orthodox medicine.**

However, the scientists' task was difficult. For many years it was illegal to dissect (cut open) dead people to find out about diseases or how the body worked. This meant they often had to rely on the old teachings of ancient Greek and Roman scientists, some of which were very wrong. For example, they thought epilepsy sufferers were possessed by demons, and that the body was governed by four liquids, or *humors:* blood, phlegm, black bile, and yellow bile.

This led to the use of many treatments that were dangerous or only worked by accident, such as using leeches to suck sick people's blood. This process was called bleeding. Sometimes large amounts of blood were drained out of patients, which weakened or even killed them.

Wise women or witches?

In any case, most people could not afford to see a doctor. Some would see a barber surgeon, who could carry out operations such as pulling out rotten teeth and amputating diseased limbs. Most relied on wise old women who remembered the ancient medicinal herbs and folk remedies. These form the basis of many of today's alternative therapies.

The Christian Church came to believe these wise women were witches, often because their treatments worked so well that they seemed to be using magic. In 1484, the Pope called for witch-hunting campaigns across Europe. From then until 1750, tens of thousands of women were burned to death. A lot of **alternative medical** knowledge was lost with them.

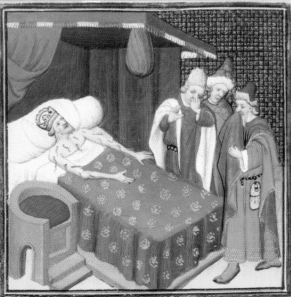

Hundreds of years ago, leeches were used to suck out the supposedly bad blood of sick people.

11

Ancient Traditions

In the rest of the world, **alternative medicines** were positively encouraged. **Acupuncture,** for example, was invented more than 4,000 years ago in China. **Ayurveda,** still widely used in India, is 5,000 years old. It is based on ancient religious texts. Like the ancient Greek theory of humors, it says that three types of energy, or *dosha,* control a person's personality, intelligence, strengths, and weaknesses. Imbalances in this energy cause illness, and the *dosha* must be restored by means of **yoga,** a **detoxifying diet, massage,** and herbs.

Massage was widely used in ancient China, Greece, and Rome. In the West, however, the Church came to frown on such intimate body contact. This means the healing power of massage has only been rediscovered in the West over the past 100 years or so.

CAM in the West

The first big development of modern CAM therapies in the West did not happen until the 1800s. Systems such as **naturopathy** and **homeopathy** were partly developed to provide gentler alternatives to grisly scientific treatments still being used, such as bleeding. Around the middle of the 1900s, however, there was a string of great medical breakthroughs that saved millions of lives. These included the development of **antibiotics** and the introduction of mass **immunization** campaigns.

While **conventional medicine** became very successful in some areas, it still could not cure common illnesses such as colds, depression, or cancer. Conventional drugs could also have horrible, long-term **side effects.** Disappointment with modern medicine in Western countries has led more and more people to look for answers in ancient and newly-developed alternative techniques. Today, CAM is more popular than ever.

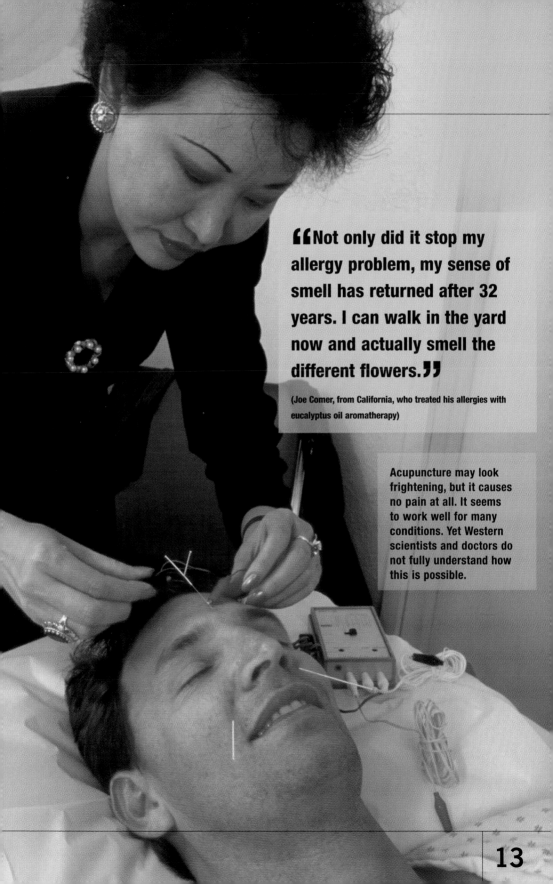

"Not only did it stop my allergy problem, my sense of smell has returned after 32 years. I can walk in the yard now and actually smell the different flowers."

(Joe Comer, from California, who treated his allergies with eucalyptus oil aromatherapy)

Acupuncture may look frightening, but it causes no pain at all. It seems to work well for many conditions. Yet Western scientists and doctors do not fully understand how this is possible.

Who Uses What?

In the United States, more than $20 billion is spent on alternative remedies each year, a little more than on **conventional medicine.** More than 40 percent of all Australians and Canadians use alternative remedies. In the United Kingdom, the figure is at least one in five.

The most frequent CAM users in the West are white, middle-class, young to middle-aged, well-educated women. The most popular treatments are relaxation techniques, **herbal medicine, massage, chiropractic,** vitamins, and **homeopathy. Hypnotherapy, acupuncture,** and **osteopathy** are also popular. Spiritual healing is popular in Holland and **reflexology** in Denmark. In Germany, doctors cannot become licensed unless they complete courses in **alternative medicine.**

Medicine in poor countries

For the 80 percent of the world's population living in poor countries, and for indigenous (native) people in developed countries, CAM is not an alternative choice: it is often the only option. India has an entire government ministry devoted to **Ayurvedic** medicine, while in Mozambique there are 80,000 **witch doctors,** but only 350 conventional doctors.

Homeopathy is one of the world's most popular types of CAM. More people use it in France than in any other country in the world.

In India, Ayurvedic medicine is the only option for many people in poor families or rural areas. As well as being affordable, it has been used for thousands of years and is well-known and trusted.

Traditional African medicine operates on principles that may seem strange to Westerners, such as the idea that disease may be caused by the spirits of angry ancestors. However, it works well for many illnesses, especially psychological ones, and uses many herbs now adopted by Western CAM, such as African prune and aloe.

In Cuba, conventional medicines are running short. This is because the U.S. government opposes the country's Communist president, Fidel Castro. It has not traded with Cuba for more than 40 years and punishes other countries that do so. Because of the lack of drugs, acupuncture is now often used as an **anesthetic** for patients during surgery so they will feel no pain. The government is also collecting knowledge from elderly people about traditional herbal remedies that are now sold in pharmacies as *medicina verde* (green medicine).

Rabies in the Philippines

The deadly disease rabies is widespread in the Philippines. People bitten by dogs can go to their local health center to have an injection to kill the virus before it reaches the brain. However, many people still rely—fatally—on cultural tradition, preferring to use *tandok* (healing stones) that they mistakenly believe can draw out the virus. Even in countries where modern Western medicine is available, it may be rejected because it is seen as foreign, and not part of the country's traditional culture.

Why Is It Used?

The general public today is better educated than ever before. Yet people are using more and more CAM treatments, many of which—according to medical researchers—have no basis in scientific fact. Why is this?

It could be partly due to people losing their faith in science, doctors, and governments following a long history of health disasters and cover-ups. For example, there were many problems with the drug thalidomide. It was given to thousands of pregnant women in the 1960s to stop morning sickness. It turned out to cause terrible deformities in their babies.

Modern medicine often seems harsh. The conventional treatment for cancer is still to "cut it (surgery), burn it (**radiotherapy**), then poison it (**chemotherapy**)," and many drugs have unpleasant **side effects.** For example, lithium, used to control the mood swings of people with **manic depression,** can also cause a person to shake uncontrollably.

Some people may feel unhappy with the way they are treated by a conventional doctor and feel they get more individual attention from a CAM practitioner.

Simple principles

Alternative remedies are seen as gentler and safer. Instead of cold, rational science based on complicated hormones, antibodies, cells, and genes, they operate on simple principles, such as preventing illness by getting the body's spirit and energy levels back into harmony.

Doctors in public healthcare systems are often too busy to spend more than a few minutes with each patient. Some say doctors do not take them seriously if they do not seem to have a "real" medical problem, such as if they just feel very tired or depressed. Alternative practitioners, meanwhile, usually spend up to an hour listening to patients' problems and firmly involve them in their own, individually-tailored healing process.

Many CAM remedies can be bought over the counter in stores. They are often cheaper than prescription drugs, although therapies involving a visit to a practitioner's office can be quite expensive. A consultation with a **homeopath** in the United States costs a patient roughly $75.

While **conventional medicine** may offer only one or two drugs for each ailment, CAM provides a huge array that can be mixed and matched until the patient finds one that suits him or her best. In addition, new remedies offering fresh hope are being discovered all the time.

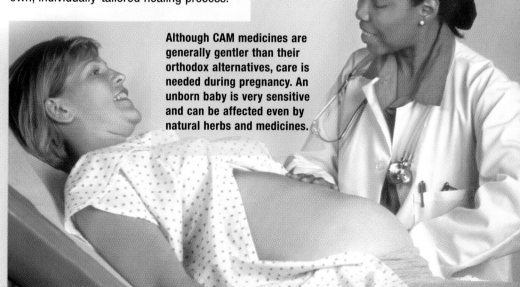

Although CAM medicines are generally gentler than their orthodox alternatives, care is needed during pregnancy. An unborn baby is very sensitive and can be affected even by natural herbs and medicines.

Looking for Miracles

CAM is often used by people suffering from life-threatening conditions such as cancer. In Western, industrialized countries, cancer affects one person in three and kills one in five. Conventional treatments, such as **radiotherapy** and **chemotherapy,** sometimes extend peoples' lives for only a few months. When conventional treatments seem to offer little hope, desperate people often look for alternatives. In Australia, more than 50 percent of cancer patients now use CAM, usually alongside **conventional medicine.** In the United States, the figure may be as high as 75 percent.

The fight against toxins

Some of the therapies may seem quite extreme. One of the most popular alternative treatments for cancer is the Gerson diet. The theory is that the disease is caused by a build-up of **toxins** in the body. These can, according to claims, be removed by consuming large amounts of fresh organic fruit and vegetables and taking vitamins. Several **enemas** using coffee are given each day. Essiac, a herb used by Native Americans, is another treatment claimed to be good at loosening up and expelling toxins from the body. Iscador, a popular treatment based on mistletoe, has shown tumor-fighting success in some studies.

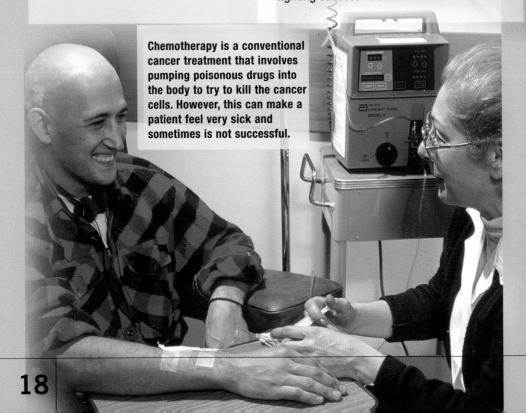

Chemotherapy is a conventional cancer treatment that involves pumping poisonous drugs into the body to try to kill the cancer cells. However, this can make a patient feel very sick and sometimes is not successful.

Such treatments may have much to offer in some cases, but there is not yet enough evidence for them to be considered miracle cures. If they were, then cancer would already have been wiped out.

Up to 30 percent of cancers may be caused by poor nutrition. Most doctors agree that a more wholesome diet can be very important, especially in preventing cancer in the first place. However, people should never go on extreme diets without seeking their doctor's advice. It could make patients who are already very ill and weak much sicker.

Eating a lot of junk food, such as burgers and fries, may make people more likely to develop serious diseases, such as cancer, later in life.

Types and Techniques

Millions of people in the Western world use the most-popular CAM therapies. But how do they actually work?

- The theory behind **acupuncture** is that illness is caused by a disruption of **chi** (life energy) that runs through the body in invisible channels called **meridians.** This can cause problems at any point along the channel. For example, a blocked stomach meridian, which also runs through the gums, could cause a toothache. To restore chi, acupuncturists insert thin needles into some of the 365 acupuncture points around the body. There is no pain, though patients may feel a slight tugging. Acupuncture can successfully treat conditions such as back pain, stress, and nausea.

❝To say, as some therapists do, that there are many and equally valid maps of the body's workings is to say that there are many and equally valid road maps of London.❞

(John Diamond, British journalist who was doubtful about CAM, in *Snake Oil and Other Preoccupations*)

Flexible steel acupuncture needles are used to tap into energy channels that practitioners believe run through the body from the head to the feet.

- **Reflexology** works on principles similar to acupuncture, but with the hand or foot viewed as a smaller reflection of the body. Practitioners restore energy flow through **massage.**

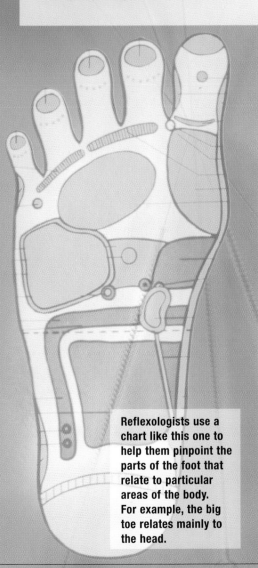

Reflexologists use a chart like this one to help them pinpoint the parts of the foot that relate to particular areas of the body. For example, the big toe relates mainly to the head.

- **Homeopathy** is based on the idea that like cures like. For example, digoxin (from the foxglove flower) is a poison that can cause heart irregularities. It is used by homeopaths to cure heart problems. However, because homeopathic remedies are so heavily diluted (like a pinch of salt in the Atlantic Ocean), the liquid is said to contain only a "memory" of the digoxin. The weaker the remedy, the greater its supposed ability to trigger the body's healing energy. A remedy may depend on the patient's **constitution,** as well as the illness. A happy, outgoing person and a nervous, withdrawn person would receive different treatment for the same disease. Homeopathy is often used to treat allergies, asthma, eczema, and anxiety. However, there is little accepted scientific evidence to show it actually works. Bach flower remedies are an offshoot of homeopathy. The 38 essences prepared from wild plants and rock water are used to affect a person's mood. One popular remedy is used to help people cope with stress, such as before exams or after an argument.

- In **herbal medicine,** plants and herbs are used to treat diseases and promote health. They are often broken down into four groups: tonics, specifics, heroics, and cleansers. Tonics, such as ginseng, slowly and gently strengthen and nourish the body. They can be taken over long periods. Specifics are stronger, and are used temporarily to deal with a particular problem. For example, echinacea is used to prevent colds. Heroics are even stronger, and must be used under supervision. Cleansers, or protectors, remove poisons from the body. An example is pectin, which is found in apples and pears.

- Faith healing involves the healer calling on God, or on other forces, such as the "higher energy of the universe," to cure a patient. Healers may channel healing power through their hands. Some studies show that sick people who are prayed for recover quicker than others, but many people doubt these results.

- **Chiropractic** theory is that many health problems stem from bad positioning of the spine and the nerves that pass through it. Chiropractors adjust segments of the backbone using anything from very fast movements to deep massage. Chiropractic is used for back pain, migraines, asthma, and sports injuries.

- **Hypnotherapy** was first practiced in ancient Egypt, where priests entered **hypnosis** through chanting. It was first popularized in the West by the Scottish doctor James Braid in the 1840s. The patient is sent into a **trance**—a deep state of relaxation—often by staring at a light or object or listening to the therapist's voice. The person is still aware of his or her surroundings, but more affected by positive suggestions made by the therapist. Hypnotherapy may help people give up smoking, overcome phobias (strong fears, such as of spiders), or become more self-confident.

Transcendental meditation

Many U.S. companies, including car manufacturing giant General Motors, now offer **transcendental meditation** (TM) classes for their employees. Research has shown that this can help people work more efficiently, take fewer sick days, feel happier in their jobs, and get along better with fellow workers.

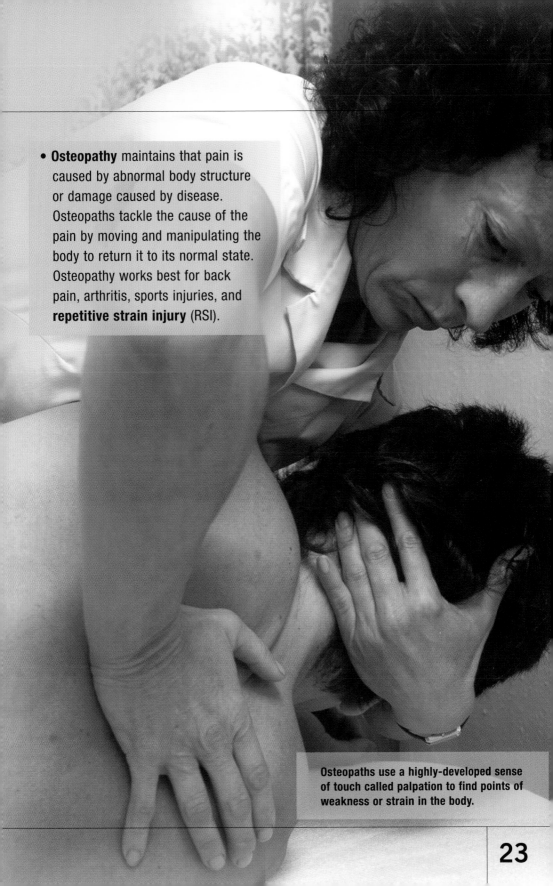

- **Osteopathy** maintains that pain is caused by abnormal body structure or damage caused by disease. Osteopaths tackle the cause of the pain by moving and manipulating the body to return it to its normal state. Osteopathy works best for back pain, arthritis, sports injuries, and **repetitive strain injury** (RSI).

Osteopaths use a highly-developed sense of touch called palpation to find points of weakness or strain in the body.

- **Massage** stimulates the nerve endings in the skin, the body's largest sense organ. This reduces levels of stress-related chemicals in the body and generally promotes a feeling of well-being. Stronger massage relieves pain. There are various kinds of massage, such as Swedish (using oils) and Japanese shiatsu, which stimulates pressure points.

- **Meditation** has been used for thousands of years in the East, but only became popular in the West in the 1960s after the British pop group, the Beatles, visited India. People who practice meditation say it is like taking a "mental bath." By concentrating on quiet, slow breathing they can calm the mind and reduce stress levels.

- Biofeedback is one of many popular relaxation techniques. Electronic devices attached to the body measure signals such as skin temperature, heart rate, and brain waves. The device beeps when, for example, the person's muscles become too tense. The person learns to relax by consciously controlling the body's reactions to stress. It is said to be good for headaches, circulation problems, and abnormal heartbeat. The Dallas Cowboys football team has used biofeedback to reduce stress and improve performance.

Fringe treatments

There are many more forms of CAM. However, scientists and practitioners of the more respected therapies may doubt that these fringe treatments work:

- Crystal healers believe the molecules (groups of atoms) in different types of crystals vibrate at different speeds. They choose the correct one to restore a sick patient's natural body vibrations to normal.

- Trepanation is the world's oldest form of surgery, dating back 7,000 years. It involves drilling a hole in a patient's skull to allow better blood circulation around the brain.

- Fans of urine therapy drink, or even bathe in, their own urine. They say urine can help build **immunity**—much like a vaccination—to conditions such as allergies, **diabetes,** and **herpes.**

- Practitioners of the Russian Buteyko Method believe that many illnesses are caused by people breathing too deeply. They claim to cure these conditions by teaching people to breathe correctly.

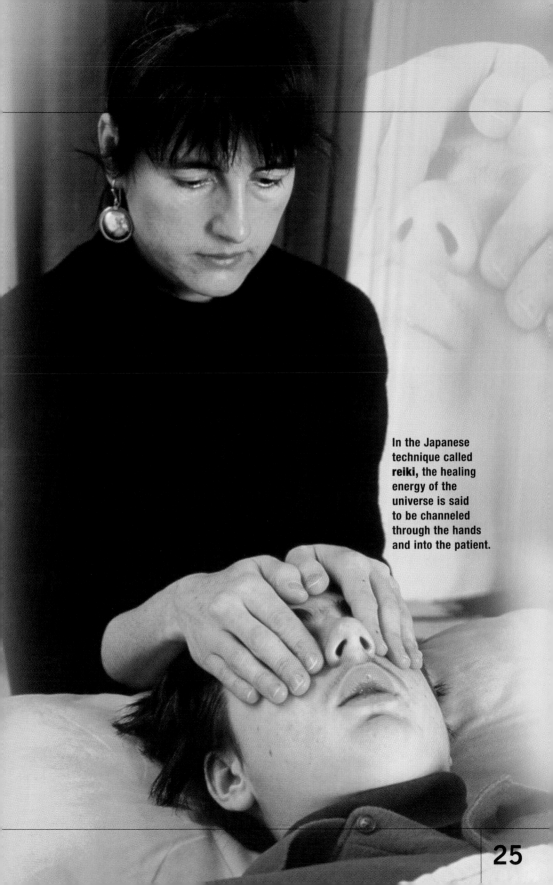

In the Japanese technique called **reiki,** the healing energy of the universe is said to be channeled through the hands and into the patient.

Marijuana

Marijuana, or cannabis, is a controversial alternative therapy. In most places it is still an illegal drug. However, marijuana has medical uses dating back thousands of years. In the 19th century, for example, Queen Victoria of Britain used it for menstrual cramps. Marijuana was not actually banned in the United States until the 1920s.

Marijuana—the benefits

Marijuana's **active ingredient** is THC—tetra-hydrocannabinol. People with many serious diseases have found that marijuana is often more helpful than prescribed drugs. For example, people with AIDS often become thin and malnourished, but find it hard to eat. They say that marijuana helps to stimulate their appetite. For people with cancer, it can help to reduce the sickness they often suffer while undergoing **chemotherapy** treatment.

Marijuana is also helpful in treating glaucoma, an eye disease. It can lower internal eye pressure associated with the disease, slowing the onset of blindness. Marijuana also seems to calm pain and muscle seizures among sufferers of **multiple sclerosis,** epilepsy, and spinal cord injuries.

Research into the benefits of marijuana is now progressing rapidly in many countries. In the United Kingdom, for example, there is an ongoing trial involving multiple sclerosis patients. If proven effective, marijuana could be available by prescription by 2004. Nevertheless, at the moment, sufferers (or their families or friends) in many countries still have to buy the drug illegally. They risk fines or imprisonment.

The medical form of marijuana is much weaker than the kind smoked by drug-users to obtain a high. It is hoped this will cut down on rare **side effects** such as hallucinations and paranoia.

The downside

Some studies have shown that marijuana may cause cancer and increase the risk of heart disease. These risks are not important for people who are terminally ill and simply want to relieve their pain. Yet antidrug campaigners say more research is needed before medical marijuana use should be allowed. They say that tighter rules are needed to prevent the law from being exploited by illegal drug abusers.

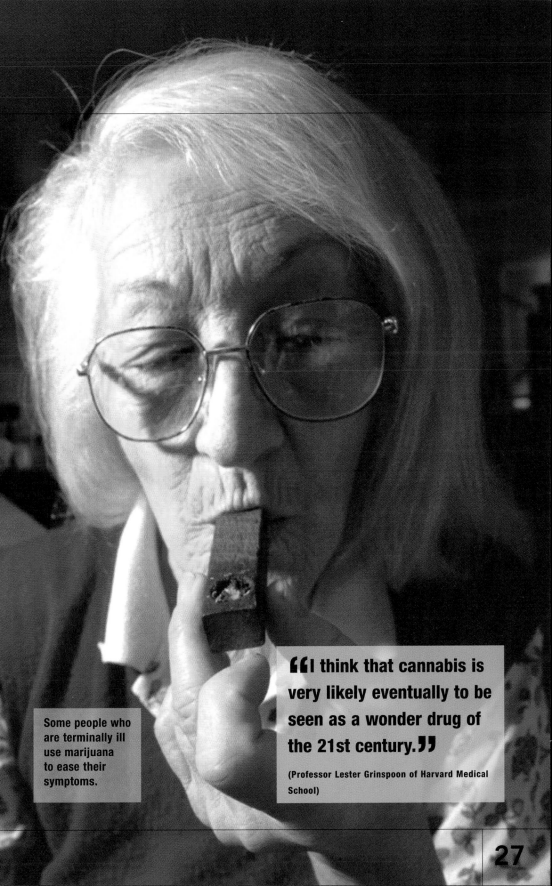

Some people who are terminally ill use marijuana to ease their symptoms.

"I think that cannabis is very likely eventually to be seen as a wonder drug of the 21st century."

(Professor Lester Grinspoon of Harvard Medical School)

Naturopathy

Naturopathy is a kind of catchall treatment that brings together many of the major alternative treatments. Hippocrates, the ancient Greek physician known as the "father of medicine," laid the foundations for it 2,500 years ago. He said that health could be maintained by the correct balance of sleep, exercise, and plain food. This idea was further developed at Austrian and German health spas in the 19th century and by the health-conscious U.S. breakfast cereal manufacturer John Kellogg.

A matter of lifestyle

Naturopaths believe more in building long-term health than fighting disease. This means naturopathy often involves an entire change of lifestyle, rather than a quick fix when people feel sick.

Naturopathy emphasizes the natural in the belief that the body can be weakened by bad diet, pollution, stress, or the lack of fresh air. Symptoms of disease are seen as signs of the body working to heal itself, and so medicines are not used to suppress or hide these symptoms. Treatments are aimed at restoring the patient's "vital force" to a point where his or her body can heal itself.

Like **Ayurveda,** naturopathic medicine relies on a wide range of treatments. These include **detoxifying diets,** exercise, herbs, **yoga, osteopathy, homeopathy,** hydrotherapy (hot and cold baths and steam treatment), **massage,** and **acupuncture.**

Regular exercise is a good way of boosting **immunity** and preventing illness.

28

Patterns or blotches on the iris of the eye may be a sign of problems elsewhere in the body.

Iridology and applied kinesiology

Some naturopaths use iridology. This involves examining the iris, the colored part of the eye. Like fingerprints, all irises are different, and changes in the pattern of the iris are thought to give information about problems inside the body. Applied kinesiology is sometimes used to diagnose allergies. The patient is asked to hold one arm out at right angles to the body, and the therapist attempts to push it back into place to judge the patient's muscle strength. The exercise is then repeated with the patient holding a potential allergen, such as pollen, in the other hand. If the person is allergic to pollen, it should be easier to push the arm down, because an allergy-causing substance is supposed to affect a person's energy. So far, there is no research evidence to support these techniques.

The Role of the Media

CAM remedies are regularly featured in news reports and advertisements in magazines or on prime-time television. Sales of CAM products usually increase following reports about therapies. This is especially true if the products are linked to a high profile celebrity, such as *Friends* star Jennifer Aniston, who used **hypnotherapy** to give up smoking, or Guns 'n' Roses singer Axl Rose, who is a big fan of **homeopathy.**

The media are important in broadening our knowledge of CAM. Most people first learn about new therapies and products—what they are good for, how to use them, and where to find them—from newspapers and television.

Miracle-cure stories

However, it is important to keep an open mind. CAM therapies may be called wonder cures. But if you read carefully, many of these stories are only about plans to conduct trials on a therapy. It is hoped it may turn out to be a wonder cure, but nothing has yet been proven. **Conventional medicine,** meanwhile, is governed by much stricter reporting regulations.

The large companies that fund medical research do not allow scientists to talk about possible new drugs until all the results have been gathered. This can take a very long time. Therefore, it can sometimes seem that modern medicine has less to offer than CAM. The media want big, dramatic stories about disasters, scandals, and miraculous medicines. Headlines such as: "Cancer—scientists still working on cure" do not sell newspapers.

Many health professionals worry about media reports of unusual cases, such as stories of people beating cancer with CAM. They fear this could even encourage people to abandon conventional treatment. CAM does seem to work well for some conditions in some circumstances. It will almost definitely turn out to have even more benefits when properly studied. However, despite hundreds of hopeful miracle-cure stories, research has not yet shown clearly that any CAM remedy can treat cancer or prevent diseases such as measles and smallpox as effectively as modern medicine and mass **immunization** programs.

Like many other Hollywood stars, Jennifer Aniston has used CAM therapies.

"Migraine headaches are really terrible. I tried a homeopathic remedy, and all I can say is 'Wow!'— what a blessing!"

(Demetrios Vouganis of Sandy, Utah, quoted on a website)

Does It Work?

With billions of dollars spent each year on CAM, why are there still so many arguments about whether or not it actually works? One reason is that many CAM treatments are taken daily over many years to slowly improve health rather than to quickly cure a specific illness.

In addition, there are many factors involved in sickness and recovery, and the body sometimes works in ways scientists cannot explain. For example, a few cancers go into **remission** for no obvious reason. Someone who had followed the Gerson diet might be convinced that he or she had been cured by CAM. This is possible but unlikely, since many people using such therapies do not recover.

Proving they work

The biggest problem is that it has not yet been possible to test many CAM remedies and to show they work as well as prescription drugs. An exception is the herb St. John's Wort, used for treating mild depression. In Germany, it outsells the antidepressant drug Prozac by a ratio of 12 to 1.

Some therapies also claim to operate on such unusual principles that it is difficult to prove their effectiveness in laboratory experiments. Some **homeopathic** remedies, for example, have often been shown to contain nothing but water and alcohol. And there is no sign of the energy channels that **acupuncturists** claim run through the body.

However, homeopathy and acupuncture do seem to work for some conditions. A possible explanation is that acupuncture actually taps into nerves and turns off pain signals in the brain. The repeated shaking involved in the preparation of homeopathic remedies might somehow change the structure of water molecules.

In any case, the failure to show clear results may not necessarily mean a product does not work. Even tests of widely-accepted conventional drugs can have conflicting results. Some big tests on Prozac, for example, have proven it works well for 80 percent of depression sufferers. Others show it has hardly any effect.

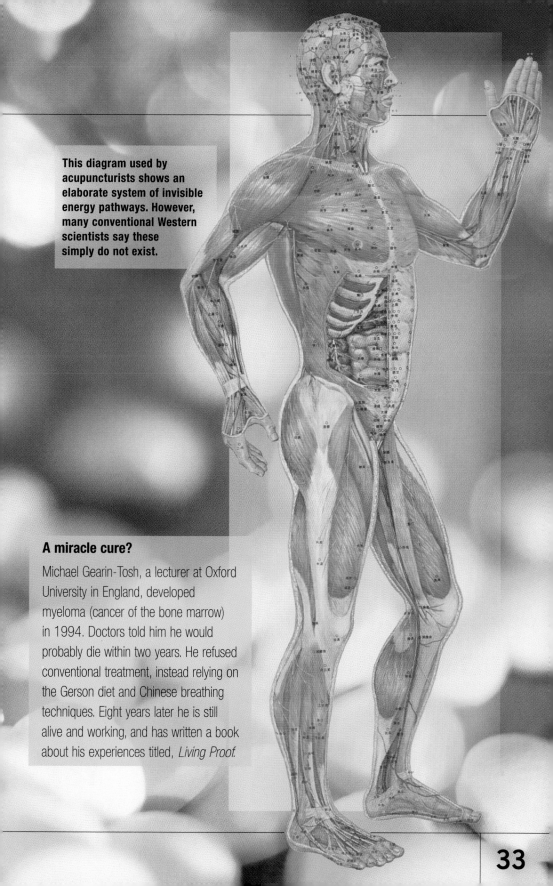

This diagram used by acupuncturists shows an elaborate system of invisible energy pathways. However, many conventional Western scientists say these simply do not exist.

A miracle cure?

Michael Gearin-Tosh, a lecturer at Oxford University in England, developed myeloma (cancer of the bone marrow) in 1994. Doctors told him he would probably die within two years. He refused conventional treatment, instead relying on the Gerson diet and Chinese breathing techniques. Eight years later he is still alive and working, and has written a book about his experiences titled, *Living Proof*.

All in the Mind?

Did you know that the human brain can produce painkilling chemicals as powerful as anything made in a laboratory? People who have suffered terrible injuries in wars and disasters sometimes do not even realize it until sometime later. Some people have even lost a limb—after being attacked by a shark or shot, for example—but felt no pain.

The powerful brain

Yoga experts can consciously alter body functions such as their heartbeat or temperature. Many people who are allergic to **anesthetics** can go through surgery after being hypnotized and feel little or no pain. Many CAM therapies, such as **massage** and **meditation,** trigger the brain to release small amounts of painkilling, feel-good chemicals called endorphins. One study on the effects of **reflexology** even found changes in the brains of rats after they had their paws massaged.

The brain clearly works in powerful ways that scientists admit they are still far from understanding. This may help to explain why some supposedly "medically impossible" alternative therapies seem to work so well, at least in some patients.

The placebo effect

A scientific phenomenon known as the **placebo effect** exists. More than 30 percent of sick people will improve if given a treatment by a doctor—even if the treatment actually contains no medicine at all. If people believe they are going to get better, their brains can sometimes actually suppress their symptoms or boost their immune system to fight off the illness. However, placebo-induced effects, unlike a genuine cure, rarely last long. Most patients quickly return to their original condition.

Positive thinking

Dr. Dean Ornish, a charming and confident doctor in the United States, reported a large decrease in heart disease among patients who followed his strict regime of diet, positive thinking, and meditation. In 2002, similar improvements were noted at eight other test sites in the country. However, the major organizations working with heart conditions in the United States did not accept that it was possible to reverse heart disease.

The aim of meditation is to relax and clear the mind. When done properly, it seems to improve people's health and could even increase their life expectancy.

The Benefits

Many conventional doctors now use CAM to treat patients for some conditions. Why do they do this? Many doctors have seen for themselves that CAM, even if it has not been scientifically proven, sometimes works better for their patients than prescription drugs. In fact, many family doctors, pain clinics, and **hospices** offer a range of the better-established therapies, such as **acupuncture, homeopathy,** and **massage.**

Psychological problems

Many of the common conditions for which doctors prescribe CAM have a psychological aspect—having to do with a person's mind and emotions. One in four people in Western countries suffer from depression at some point in their lives. Many others are hit by anxiety, stress at work, and panic attacks. If untreated, these can go on to become the root of other common complaints, such as migraines, high blood pressure, unexplained pains, and digestive problems.

Because CAM works **holistically,** it is often much better than **conventional medicine** at dealing with all the underlying causes of a problem. As the **placebo effect** shows, the mind has a great deal of control over the body's healing processes. Unlike busy doctors, practitioners spend a long time talking to their patients and help them to unlock their own healing powers. This can be much more successful than a doctor's pills for people whose problems stem from depression or stress.

Physical problems

CAM works well for many purely physical complaints, too. More and more people now do little exercise and work in front of a computer all day. Back pain, **repetitive strain injury,** and other physical problems are becoming more common. Massage, acupuncture, and **osteopathy** can often treat these more successfully than painkillers.

Work-related stress is a problem that affects nearly everybody at some time or another. If untreated, it can go on to cause a wide range of physical problems.

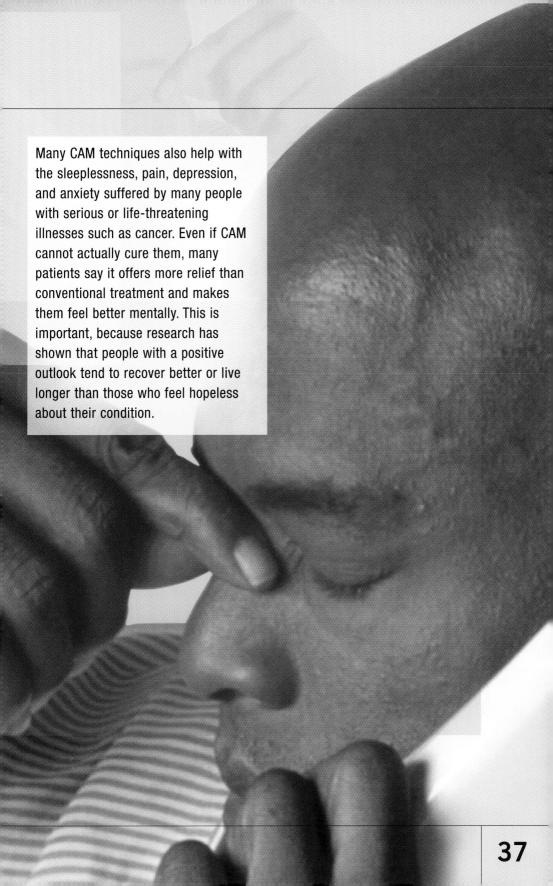

Many CAM techniques also help with the sleeplessness, pain, depression, and anxiety suffered by many people with serious or life-threatening illnesses such as cancer. Even if CAM cannot actually cure them, many patients say it offers more relief than conventional treatment and makes them feel better mentally. This is important, because research has shown that people with a positive outlook tend to recover better or live longer than those who feel hopeless about their condition.

Curing Body and Spirit

The relationship between **conventional** and **alternative medicine** has traditionally been hostile. Several years ago, the *British Medical Journal* described **chiropractic** treatments as no more useful than the "examination of a bird's entrails." (Ancient peoples thought they could foretell the future by looking at the innards of dead animals.) But things are changing. Today, most CAM is actually used in a **complementary** way with conventional medicine. For example, a person may use **homeopathy** to calm his or her nerves before surgery.

Mind, body, and spirit

Doctors now increasingly realize that many patients want and need treatment for their spirit as well as their body. Conventional medicine usually does not provide this emotional and spiritual backup. Many doctors now accept CAM techniques as long as they do not compete with or replace conventional treatment. At least 40 percent of hospitals in Europe, and even more **hospices** and pain clinics, now offer complementary therapies to help increase the success of a patient's treatment.

Traditional healing

In the United States, successful programs for treating alcoholism among Native Americans mix psychiatric counseling with traditional healing arts. These include chanting, smudging (burning sage or scented woods), sweat lodges, and dream interpretation. The drug peyote, which makes people hallucinate, is sometimes used, too.

The Bristol Cancer Help Centre

The Bristol Cancer Help Centre in the United Kingdom has been a pioneer in this area. The center's philosophy is that each person's journey with cancer is unique. The World Health Organization says the Centre represents "the gold standard for complementary care in cancer." In addition to the patient's conventional treatment program, staff members devise an individual plan of relaxation, **meditation, visualization,** music or art therapy, spiritual healing, and **massage.** These are called psycho-neuro immunology (PNI) therapies. The staff works together with the patient's doctors to make sure no therapy will interfere with his or her medical treatment.

Many studies have shown that these therapies can greatly improve on conventional treatment alone. They may help create natural killer cells in the body that destroy unhealthy cancer cells. People who have received PNI treatment certainly tend to be happier and more relaxed, live longer, cope better with the trauma of a life-threatening illness, and recover faster from treatments such as **chemotherapy.**

The Bristol Cancer Help Centre looks after every aspect of a patient's needs. It provides peaceful gardens where people can relax and quality meals packed full of healthy ingredients to help sick people get better.

The Dangers

An estimated 130,000 Americans die each year from the **side effects** of prescription drugs. CAM products are generally much safer. However, nothing is risk-free. Kava kava, a herb used to treat anxiety, has been linked to liver failure. Gingko biloba, used to boost brain power, and echinacea, used to prevent colds, could reduce fertility.

The quality of herbs

One problem is that the quality of herbs can vary greatly depending on the soil and the climate in which they were grown, and how they are stored. In 1998, the *Los Angeles Times* tested ten popular brands of St. John's Wort. Three had less than half the strength listed on the label. **Complementary medicines** may also interact with **conventional medicines** in dangerous ways. St. John's Wort, garlic, and gingko biloba can stop blood-thinning drugs from working properly. St. John's Wort may also affect the contraceptive pill and medicines for asthma, epilepsy, and migraine. Some products might also be contaminated. Lead, arsenic, and mercury were found in one-third of Asian herbs tested in California in 1998.

Dangerous practices

Although most people in the United States get enough vitamins from their diet, some people take megadoses for their supposed health benefits. Occasionally they end up poisoning themselves. Because their bodies are smaller, children are at greatest risk of overdose. Even therapies that do not involve swallowing products are not 100 percent safe. For example, **hypnotherapy** could be dangerous for those who are depressed or epileptic.

However, the biggest danger is not from using CAM therapies, but from not using conventional treatment. For example, relying on faith healing alone can be very dangerous. There have been many cases of people dying from easily-curable diseases after refusing conventional medical treatment. In 1996, several children in Germany died after **homeopaths** told their parents to stop giving them insulin for **diabetes.** This condition can be kept under control with conventional drugs. The homeopathic remedies were themselves harmless, but the treatment (or lack of it) killed the children.

Garlic—the pros and cons

Garlic is often taken by HIV sufferers to stop the build-up of **cholesterol** that is caused by their medication. In 2001, researchers at the U.S. National Institutes of Health found that garlic had the unwanted side effect of massively reducing the levels of important anti-HIV drugs in the blood.

Healers or Fakers?

Many CAM practitioners, such as **osteopaths** and Chinese herbalists, study at colleges and universities. Yet others can train in just a couple of months and may have very little medical knowledge. In a British trial of **reflexologists** in 2000, not one could diagnose six common illnesses when unable to talk to the patients.

Tapping into fears

Unfortunately, not all people selling CAM products are who they seem to be. Some take advantage of sick or frightened people, selling them useless remedies to get rich quick. Within days of the terrorist attacks of September 11, 2001, nearly 200 websites sprang up claiming their **herbal** remedies could cure the deadly disease anthrax. At the time, it was feared terrorists might release the germs causing this very infectious disease to kill thousands of people. However, anthrax can kill in days—much too fast for oregano oil or zinc water to work. The only known treatment for anthrax is very strong **antibiotics.**

Operation Cure All

The U.S. Federal Trade Commission launched Operation Cure All in 1997 to crack down on Internet companies making such false claims. However, the Internet is hard to police, and anyone surfing the Net should be wary. Warning bells should ring if a product claims to be a panacea, or cure-all, capable of clearing up anything from baldness to heart disease. Panaceas do not exist. Also troubling are products that claim to have "secret ingredients" or ads that include the amazing success stories of unnamed patients. These are easy to invent. Health frauds also often talk of secret government plots to suppress their miracle cure.

"Your very first capsule will start to melt down fat just like hot water melts down ice!"

(Claim made by the manufacturers of an alternative weight loss pill—despite this being a physical impossibility)

Therapeutic Touch

In 1998, Colorado student Emily Rosa greatly embarrassed practitioners of Therapeutic Touch (TT), who claim to sense and heal the human "energy field." In an experiment, Emily showed they could not sense anything at all when a barrier stopped them from seeing whether or not a patient was actually in front of them. The practitioners complained that Emily had blocked their powers with her "negative energy." U.S. magician James Randi has offered one million dollars to anyone who can prove that TT actually works. So far, no one has been able to do so.

Radionics

One questionable CAM therapy is radionics. Practitioners claim to use psychic powers and a mysterious black box to heal the sick and give advice on everything from gambling to animal breeding—sometimes from hundreds of miles away. U.S. practitioner Shelvie Rettman was convicted of fraud in 1998 after advising a cancer patient to stop **chemotherapy.** The patient, who was charged $2,000 for the bogus treatment, died soon afterwards.

It is important to be careful when using the Internet to find out about CAM treatments. Information may seem convincing, but could be misleading or even completely false.

The Need for Research

Despite their popularity, CAM products are still up for debate, simply because few have been tested in the kind of trials that mainstream drugs must undergo to prove that they work. In fact, most good practitioners would like their therapy to be properly tested. Then everyone could see, once and for all, that it is effective. However, many manufacturers are small firms lacking enough money to do such testing.

Drug companies

Big **pharmaceutical** companies are usually not interested in testing CAM, as natural products cannot have a **patent** taken out on them. In fact, some CAM manufacturers believe the big drug companies are actively blocking research. Natural alternatives, if scientifically proven, could pose dangerous competition to their chemical products. There has traditionally been little interest from governments, either. They have not been willing to spend taxpayers' money on researching remedies unlikely to be dramatically effective.

Government research

However, with at least one in five people in Western countries using CAM, the lack of research benefits only those who get rich from patients' ignorance. Some much-needed research is now finally being done. The budget of the U.S. government's National Center for **Complementary and Alternative Medicine** (NCCAM) rose from $2 million in 1993 to more than $100 million in 2002. Australia has a Complementary Medicines Evaluation Committee (CMEC). In Canada, the government set up an Office of Natural Health Products in 1999. It is working to ensure the safety of CAM products.

Yet the amount spent on researching CAM is a tiny fraction of the amount spent on **conventional medical** research. In the United Kingdom, for example, the Department of Health in 2002 spent only 0.08 percent of its annual research budget on CAM. To prove their worth in tests, CAM products must show they work better than a **placebo** and have no dangerous **side effects.** Large trials involving hundreds of people are needed, not just individual success stories.

"A potentially powerful resource is at our fingertips, but its benefits will be limited ... unless somewhere, somehow, purses are opened and funds dedicated to its systematic study."

(Britain's Prince Charles, who in 2000 tried to persuade the British government to spend $15 million on a five-year CAM research program)

Herbs and the Environment

People now use more than 700 **herbal** remedies. The raw products for some, such as St. John's Wort, are grown and harvested at massive farms. Yet up to 90 percent are still harvested from the wild. Many people mistakenly think wild herbs are better than farmed herbs. This has led to many popular North American and European herb species, including arnica and echinacea, to become endangered through over-collection.

Although licenses are now needed to harvest many North American and European herbs, many in the developing world are still threatened, often by loss of habitat. Nearly one-third of all our medicines come from plants. Scientists believe we are most likely to find cures for cancer and AIDS in the millions of plants in the world's tropical rain forests. However, without protection, the rain forests could disappear by the year 2015.

Ethno-medicine

There could also be great potential, for both **conventional medicine** and CAM, in ethno-medicine. This comes from traditional remedies used by people of the world's remote mountains, jungles, and deserts. In fact, many of today's CAM treatments have been discovered in this way. **Reiki,** for example, was developed by a Japanese man who based it on ancient Tibetan traditions. Practitioners use their hands to channel healing reiki ("universal energy" in Japanese) into the patient's body.

Meanwhile, Native American sweat lodges have become popular in many parts of the United States. Hot and steamy, they are used to cleanse the skin, calm the mind, and keep disease at bay. Western doctors today also often advise flu patients to breathe in steam to remove the infection from their lungs.

With so many diseases that still cannot be fully cured, we could learn much by studying techniques that have been used by people around the world over thousands of years.

Indigenous peoples around the world often have their own ways of treating diseases. Some of these may turn out to work better than the methods used in the West today.

Oils for aches and pains

Australian Aborigines have always used tea tree oil. Trials in 1923 showed it was an effective antiseptic, so it was issued to Australian soldiers in World War II. The European settlers also borrowed the Aborigines' goanna oil, a mixture of eucalyptus, pine, mint, and menthol used for aches and pains. Today, scientists are asking the Aborigines about many of their other traditional remedies in the hope of discovering other useful medicines.

Legal Matters

Manufacturers of medical drugs are governed by strict regulations. However, few types of CAM are classified as medicines because they have not been proven effective in clinical trials accepted by government scientists. In the United States, therefore, herbs are seen as food supplements and do not have to be screened by the Federal Drug Administration (FDA) to prove they are safe.

Fair trade rules

In fact, the only laws governing many CAM products are fair trade rules about making false claims—the same as those applied to used car salespeople. There is evidence, for example, that St. John's Wort may work as well as **conventional medicines** to help fight depression. Yet the label on the bottle can only say: "Helps support a positive mood."

Regulation

The regulation of practitioners in the United States varies from state to state. **Naturopaths** are licensed in 11 states, **acupuncturists** in 34, and **chiropractors** in all 50. In Canada, only licensed physicians may practice **homeopathy.** In Australia, the National Herbalists Association of Australia (NHAA) was founded in 1920 to maintain minimum standards. There are twelve colleges teaching the subject. To ensure quality and safety, the Australian government has set up a **Complementary Medicines** Evaluation Committee.

In the United Kingdom, there is little regulation at all. People can set themselves up as practitioners as long as they do not practice dentistry, deliver babies, treat sexually-transmitted diseases, or work as veterinarians. However, **osteopaths** and chiropractors must now be trained and qualified to a minimum standard.

These students of **reflexology** will spend several years learning how to treat people. Yet others may learn in just a few weeks. This is hardly enough time to cover the basics, and they may end up doing more harm than good.

The Department of Health will soon also start regulating acupuncture, **herbal medicine,** and possibly some other therapies. In most other European countries, only medical doctors can offer CAM and they must have a government license. Germany gives licenses to thousands of *Heilpraktiker* (naturopathic healers), as long as they pass a test in basic medical knowledge. Most legitimate practitioners want to be regulated, because it means they can control the prices of treatment and provide a high standard of service.

Marijuana

In 2001, Canada became the first country to decriminalize marijuana for medical use, meaning people could use it if they were very ill. Patients, who need a photo identity card and permission from their doctor, can either grow their own or buy it from government-licensed farms. Some U.S. states, such as California, have also legalized medical marijuana. However, possessing it is still illegal under federal law. Patients could, in theory, be prosecuted.

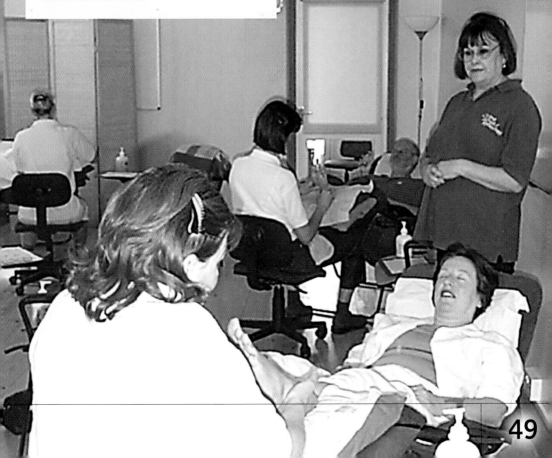

People to Talk To

In the world of CAM, it can sometimes be difficult to know who are legitimate practitioners, how much to pay, or how to make sense of the huge range of information available.

Books and websites

It is important to listen to both sides of the debate. Information in books written by experts is likely to be more reliable than information on unofficial Internet sites. The best books may be those written by medical doctors or those that state that they have been "peer reviewed." This means the facts or research have been checked and approved by health professionals.

Doctors

A good doctor will know about the potential risks and **side effects** of the more common CAM techniques. Some doctors may be against the idea of CAM or may not know a great deal about a specific therapy. In this case, a patient may choose another doctor who is more open-minded. However, it is always important to get a medical diagnosis before deciding whether CAM is appropriate. A doctor should be kept informed of any CAM therapies a patient is using.

Practitioners

Practitioners can give detailed information about their particular therapy. However, many therapists do not have to meet the same minimum standards as doctors. It is a good idea to check out their qualifications, their years of experience, and whether they are licensed. It is also a good idea to get information from them in writing. A good practitioner will not suggest the wrong treatment or advise avoiding **conventional medicine** for serious conditions.

Other organizations

Many people find it useful to talk to a charity or organization related to their disease or health condition. These often have the most up-to-date information on research and good CAM alternatives to conventional medicine. Government offices dealing with natural remedies or fair trade offices can give advice about products that are potentially dangerous or have been banned. They will know about practitioners who have had legal action taken against them. Pharmacists can help explain the level of **active ingredients** in herbs and vitamins and whether these are strong enough to have any effect.

It is often useful to speak to other people who have used the practitioner or therapy and find out about their experiences. National professional organizations devoted to the therapy in question are also usually able to provide lists of the best practitioners.

Information and Advice

The following organizations, groups, websites, and books can provide excellent information and advice on CAM, from all sides of the debate.

CAM contacts

Alternative Medicine Foundation, Inc.
P.O. Box 60016
Potomac, MD 20859
(301) 340-1960
http://www.amfoundation.org
This foundation provides objective information on therapies and practitioners. It's goal is to integrate alternative and conventional medicine.

Foundation for the Advancement of Innovative Medicine
Two Executive Blvd.
Suffern, NY 10601
(518) 758-7967; (877) 634-3246
http://www.faim.org
FAIM describes "innovative medicine" as a treatment or theory that is outside the mainstream. They believe that innovative medicine can and should be complementary to conventional medicine. Among FAIM's goals are to educate the public on the benefits and issues of innovative medicine and to encourage research and development of innovative medicine.

National Center for Complementary and Alternative Medicine (NCCAM)
NCCAM Clearinghouse
P.O. Box 7923
Gaithersburg, MD 20898
(301) 519-3153; (888) 644-6226
http://www.nccam.nih.gov
The NCCAM supports research on complementary and alternative medicine; trains researchers in CAM; and provides information to the public and to professionals on which CAM works, which CAM does not work, and why.

National Foundation for Alternative Medicine
1629 K Street NW, Suite 402
Washington, D.C. 20006
(202) 463-4900
http://www.nfam.org
NFAM's mission is to seek out effective complementary and alternative treatments not easily accessible or unavailable in the U.S.; evaluate treatments; and report their findings to the general public.

More Books to Read

Kowalski, Kathiann M. *Alternative Medicine: Is It for You?* Berkeley Heights, N.J.: Enslow Publishers, 1998.

Pascoe, Elaine. *Mysteries of the Rainforest: 20th Century Medicine Man.* Farmington Hills, Mich.: Blackbirch Press, Inc., 1997.

Rattenbury, Jeanne. *Understanding Alternative Medicine.* Danbury, Conn.: Franklin Watts, 1999.

Steinfeld, Alan. *Careers in Alternative Medicine.* New York: Rosen Publishing Group, Inc., 2000.

Glossary

active ingredient ingredient in a medicine that acts on the body

acupuncturist person who practices *acupuncture*—to heal by placing needles at certain points in the body

alternative medicine medicine that is not scientifically proven

anesthetic drug given to make a person go numb in a certain part of the body, or go into a deep sleep

antibiotic medicine that can destroy or prevent the growth of bacteria and cure infections

Ayurveda ancient Indian medical system based on the idea that illness is caused by an imbalance of the different types of energy in the body

chemotherapy chemicals given to cancer patients to help kill cancer cells

chi life energy that some CAM practitioners believe runs through the body in channels

chiropractic treatment in which the spine is adjusted to help cure health problems; a person who practices chiropractics is a *chiropractor*

cholesterol type of fat that can build up inside blood vessels due to a bad diet and little exercise

complementary medicine medicine that is used in conjunction with conventional medicine to treat aspects of an illness that conventional medicine may not be able to deal with easily

constitution description of a person according to their physical and personality type

conventional medicine medicine practiced by most doctors and hospitals in the Western world; also known as orthodox medicine

detoxifying diet diet for flushing out toxins or poisons from the body

diabetes disease that makes people unable to break down sugar in their bodies. Many diabetics have to inject a hormone called insulin each day.

enema liquid forced into someone's anus through a hose or tube to clean out his or her intestines

herbal medicine herbs and plants used to treat diseases and promote health

herpes virus that can cause cold sores on the lips and blisters on the body

holistic treatment treatment for the whole person, rather than just the symptoms of the illness

homeopathy treatment based on using tiny amounts of natural products to promote healing in the body

hospice special hospital for terminally-ill people

hypnosis state of deep relaxation in which a person can still see, hear, and follow commands

hypnotherapy treatment involving hypnosis to treat a patient

immunity body's ability to fight off infections and diseases. *Immunization* makes people immune to a disease, usually through an injection.

manic depression disorder that causes extreme mood swings, from feeling very happy to very depressed; also known as bipolar affective disorder

massage rubbing and pressing a person's body to reduce muscle and joint pain and improve overall physical and mental health

meditation ancient Eastern practice in which people concentrate on a word, a light, or an idea and clear their minds to focus on their breathing

meridian invisible energy channel that acupuncturists believe run through the body

multiple sclerosis disease of the nervous system that can cause muscle stiffness, shaking, pain, and tiredness

naturopathy way **of buildin**g up health and energy through diet, exercise, and a healthy lifestyle

orthodox medicine *see* conventional medicine

osteopathy treatment of illness and pain by pressing and moving the bones and muscles

patent official right to control and receive income from an invention

pharmaceutical having to do with making and selling drugs

placebo effect when people's symptoms disappear after receiving treatment that contains no medication

radiotherapy radiation therapy given to cancer patients to reduce the size of tumors

reflexology system of massage of the hand or foot used to relieve tension and treat illness; a person who practices reflexology is a *reflexologist*

reiki type of healing in which a practitioner channels healing energy into a patient's body

remission stage where a cancerous tumor or other disorder seems to disappear or stop growing or spreading. If a patient is in remission for five years, he or she is usually said to be cured.

repetitive strain injury type of injury common in people who strain their muscles by repeating the same movements for long periods

side effect additional, and usually negative, effect of a drug

toxin poisonous substance taken in by the body, such as from smoking or eating vegetables treated with pesticides

trance state of very deep relaxation entered during hypnotherapy

transcendental meditation method of detaching oneself from problems by meditating and chanting

visualization use of special meditation techniques, such as picturing a tumor getting smaller

witch doctor traditional medicine man or woman who often combines magical practices with alternative medicine

yoga system of body and breathing exercises used for relaxation and the development of strength and flexibility

Index

A acupuncture 4, 13, 20, 32, 36, 54
    conventional doctors 36
    Cuba 15
    energy channels 32, 33
    history 12
    naturopathy 28
    regulation 48, 49
    users 14
 AIDS 26, 46
 allergies 13, 21, 24, 29
 applied kinesiology 29
 aromatherapy 13
 asthma 4, 21, 22, 40
 Ayurveda 8, 12, 14, 15, 54

B Bach flower remedies 21
 biofeedback 24
 bleeding 11
 Buteyko Method 24

C cancer 5, 16, 18, 19, 32, 37
    alternative therapies 18
    complementary care 38, 39
    conventional medicine 12
    diet 19, 28, 33, 39
    marijuana 26
    remission 32
 chemotherapy 16, 18, 26, 39, 43, 54
 chiropractic 8, 14, 22, 38, 48, 54
 conventional medicine 6, 7, 12, 15, 16, 17, 30,
    36, 38
 crystal healing 8, 24

D depression 4, 12, 32, 36, 37

E echinacea 22, 40, 46
 energy therapies 8
 ethno-medicine 46, 47

F faith healing 8, 22, 41

G Gerson diet 18, 32, 33
 ginseng 8, 22

H herbal medicine 8, 10, 11, 22, 54
    claims 42
    Cuba 15
    dangers 40
    regulation 49
    use 14, 46
 holistic treatment 6
 homeopathy 8, 12, 14, 21, 30, 31, 54
    conventional medicine 36, 38
    media 30
    migraine 31
    naturopathy 28
    regulation 48
    tests 32

H hypnotherapy 4, 8, 30, 34, 41, 54
    media 30
    theory 22
    users 14

I immunization 12, 30, 54
 Internet remedy sales 42, 43
 iridology 29

M marijuana 26, 27, 49
 massage 8, 12, 24, 36, 55
    cancer 39
    chiropractic 22
    conventional doctors 36
    naturopathy 28
    painkilling 34
    reflexology 21
    users 14
 meditation 5, 6, 35, 55
    cancer 39
    mind-body systems 8
    painkilling 34
    theory 24
    transcendental 22

N naturopathy 12, 28, 29, 48, 55

O orthodox medicine 10 (*see* conventional medicine)
 osteopathy 8, 23, 36, 55
    naturopathy 28
    regulation 48
    users 14

P placebo effect 34, 36, 55

R radionics 43
 radiotherapy 16, 18, 55
 reflexology 14, 21, 34, 48, 55
 reiki 8, 25, 46, 55
 research into CAM 44, 45

S spiritual healing 14, 39
 St. John's Wort 4, 32, 40, 46, 48

T Therapeutic Touch 43
 Traditional Chinese Medicine 8
 transcendental meditation 22
 trepanation 10, 24

U urine therapy 4, 24

V vitamins 6, 14, 41, 50

W witch doctors 14, 55
 witches 11

Y yoga 6, 8, 9, 12, 28, 34, 55